PIANO/VOCAL SELECTIONS

CATS

MUSIC FROM THE MOTION PICTURE SOUNDTRACK

T0066256

ISBN 978-1-5400-8673-0

HAL•LEONARD®

Visit Hal Leonard Online at
www.halleonard.com

Contact us:
Hal Leonard
7777 West Bluemound Road
Milwaukee, WI 53213
Email: info@halleonard.com

In Europe, contact:
Hal Leonard Europe Limited
42 Wigmore Street
Marylebone, London, W1U 2RN
Email: info@halleonardeurope.com

In Australia, contact:
Hal Leonard Australia Pty. Ltd.
4 Lentara Court
Cheltenham, Victoria, 3192 Australia
Email: info@halleonard.com.au

CONTENTS

JELLICLE SONGS FOR JELLICLE CATS

Music by ANDREW LLOYD WEBBER
Text by TREVOR NUNN
and RICHARD STILGOE after T.S. ELIOT

Moderately fast

Are you blind when you're born? __ Can you

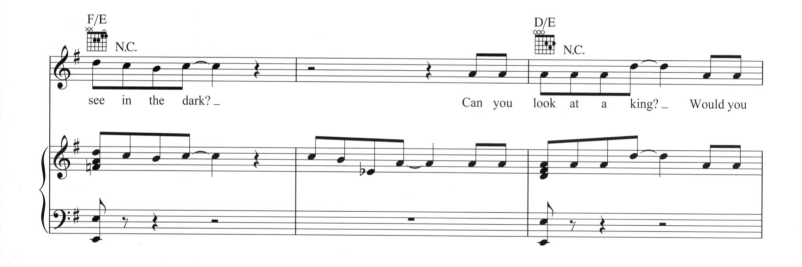

see in the dark? __ Can you look at a king? __ Would you

sit on his throne? __ Can you say of your bite __ that it's

THE OLD GUMBIE CAT

Music by ANDREW LLOYD WEBBER
Text by T.S. ELIOT

To Coda ⊕

THE RUM TUM TUGGER

Music by ANDREW LLOYD WEBBER
Text by T.S. ELIOT

art - ful and know-ing.   The Rum Tum Tug - ger does-n't care for a cud - dle, but I'll

leap up - on your lap   in the mid-dle of your sew-ing, for there's noth-ing I en-joy like a hor-ri-ble mud-dle.

BUSTOPHER JONES: THE CAT ABOUT TOWN

Music by ANDREW LLOYD WEBBER
Text by T.S. ELIOT

MUNGOJERRIE AND RUMPLETEAZER

Music by ANDREW LLOYD WEBBER
Text by T.S. ELIOT

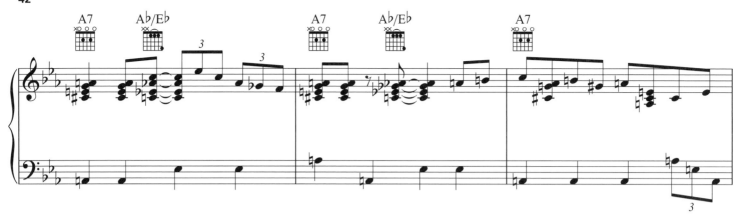

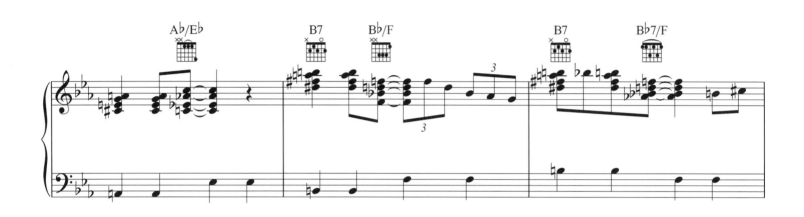

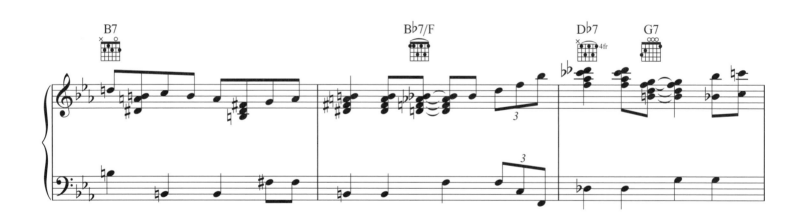

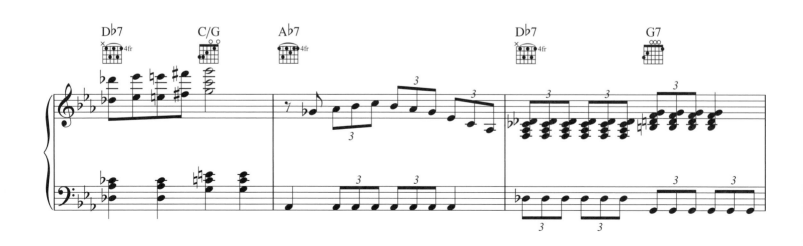

Mun - go - jer - rie and Rum - ple - teaz - er have a ver - y un - us - u - al gift of the gab. We are

high - ly ef - fi - cient cat bur - glers as well and re - mark - a - bly smart at a smash and grab. We

make our home in Vic - to - ri - a Grove, we have no reg - u - lar oc - cu - pa - tion. We are

plau - si - ble fel - lows who like to en - gage a friend - ly po - lice - man in con - ver -

OLD DEUTERONOMY

Music by ANDREW LLOYD WEBBER
Text by T.S. ELIOT

BEAUTIFUL GHOSTS

Words and Music by TAYLOR SWIFT
and ANDREW LLOYD WEBBER

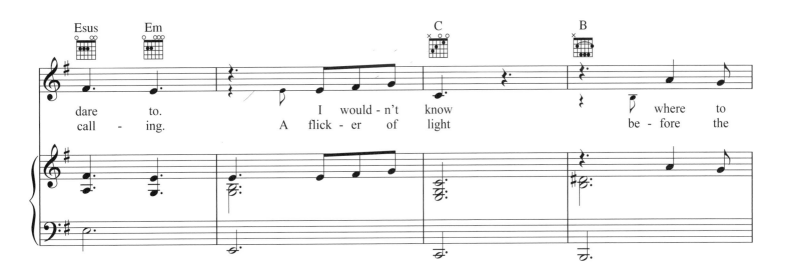

phan - toms of night. And I know that this life is - n't safe, but it's wild and it's

free.

D.S. al Coda

CODA

ghosts.

And the

mem - 'ries were lost long a - go,

so I'll

dance with these beau - ti - ful ghosts.

cresc.   molto rit.   *f* a tempo   rit.

GUS: THE THEATRE CAT

Music by ANDREW LLOYD WEBBER
Text by T.S. ELIOT

Gracefully

Gus is the
Cat at the The-a-tre Door. My name as I ought to have
coat's ver-y shab-by, I'm thin as a rake, and I suf-fer from pal-sy, which

told you be-fore, is real-ly As-par-a-gus. But that's such a
makes my paw shake. Yet I was, in my youth,_ quite the smart-est of

SKIMBLESHANKS: THE RAILWAY CAT

Music by ANDREW LLOYD WEBBER
Text by T.S. ELIOT

MACAVITY: THE MYSTERY CAT

Music by ANDREW LLOYD WEBBER
Text by T.S. ELIOT

MR. MISTOFFELEES

Music by ANDREW LLOYD WEBBER
Text by T.S. ELIOT

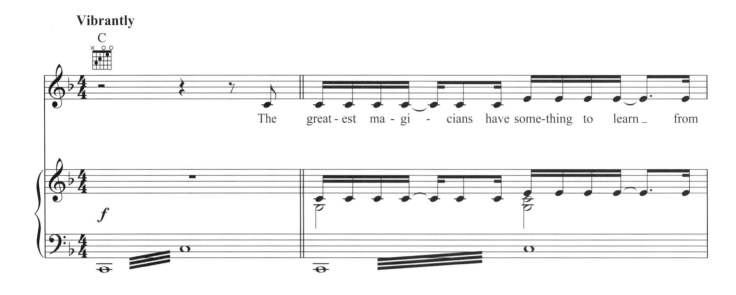

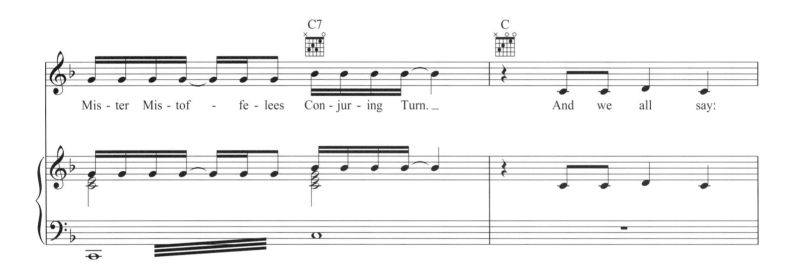

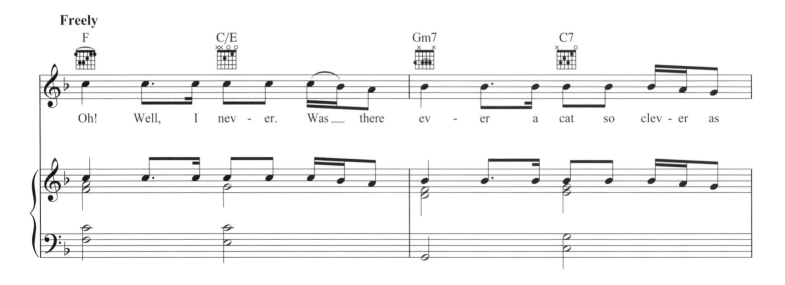

Tempo I

MEMORY

Music by ANDREW LLOYD WEBBER
Text by TREVOR NUNN after T.S. ELIOT

leave me _____ all a-lone with the mem - ory _____ of my days in the

sun. _____ If you touch me you'll un - der - stand what

hap - pi - ness is. Look a new day has be - gun.

THE AD-DRESSING OF CATS

Music by ANDREW LLOYD WEBBER
Text by T.S. ELIOT

Moderate Admirable March

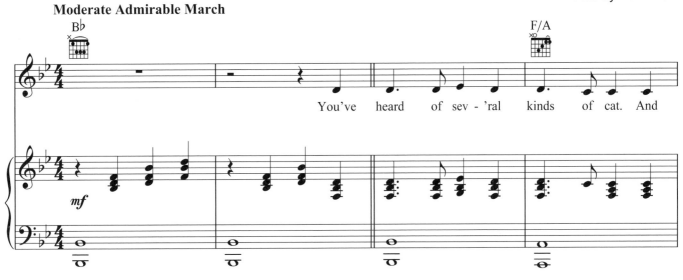

You've heard of sev-'ral kinds of cat. And

my o-pin-ion now is that you should need no ___ in-ter-pret-er to

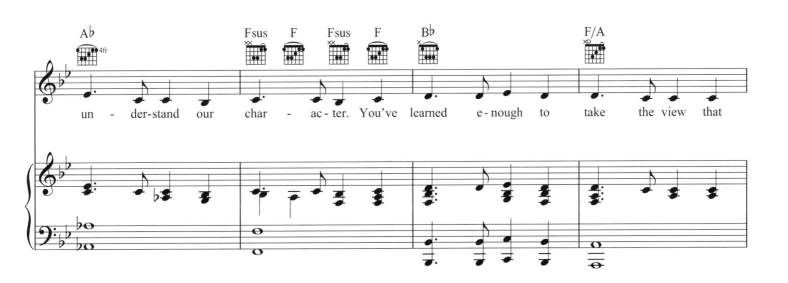

un-der-stand our char-ac-ter. You've learned e-nough to take the view that